LOVER MOT

Poems about Love, Motherhood & Everything Else Women Transcend

By Frances M. Thompson

First Edition: Published November 2020

Dedicated to the women we were,
the women we are, and the women we will be.

Contents

5

Introduction

I used to hate poetry. It was one of many things force-fed to me at school, and therefore, was quickly and generously tarnished with my disinterest and disdain. It interrupted more enjoyable English literature lessons where I got to write my own stories or read those of others, and I strongly suspect poetry was one of the main reasons I didn't go on to study English Language or Literature beyond the age of 16. Instead, I rather symbolically turned my back on this language I loved by opting for two foreign languages at A-Level, French and German. However, this was a thinly-veiled act of rebellion because, of course, my fascination persisted, bubbling through the study of other people's words and rhythms, along with my third subject choice, Theatre Studies, where I got to bring words and stories to life by acting and directing.

Why did I hate poetry at school? Well, it didn't look like the poetry I have since discovered. It came across as restrictive (with its secret set of structures I didn't understand), elitist (we studied Seamus Heaney, W.B. Yeats and Lord Byron, all old white men I couldn't relate to), and it required so much in-depth discussion and dissection of sentences (my own pen being told to massacre each line) that any impact or sensation I felt was so heavily laboured it just didn't seem worth it when I could pick up a book or switch on the TV and get instant entertainment and gratification from a novel or soap opera.

Also, I was 14, 15, 16, and I wanted to spend as much time as possible with my friends, making each other laugh, chasing unsuitable boys, and later figuring out how we could obtain enough alcohol to feel its effects on a Friday night after school. There was also the incentive of studying foreign languages meaning more trips abroad, and so foreign boys to chase and foreign booze to drink too!

Fast forward two decades (which of course is nothing like a fast or forward experience) and I have fallen clumsily, hopelessly, and happily in love with poetry.

It didn't happen like most of my real-life love affairs where I too often fell hurriedly - hard and heavy, and usually in a heap on top of myself - but rather slowly and steadily with more than a few stop-starts.

It's also true that many people held my hand on this path to true love.

There was the emergence of #instapoetry and its wild popularity thanks to the likes of Rupi Kaur, Warsan Shire, Yrsa Daley-Ward - all young women (of colour) who wrote about their bodies, their pain, and their relationships with smart, succinct prose that had few words, but huge impact.

There was a fellow new mother I met one day in a cafe close to my house on a cold spring morning as I wrangled with my seven-month-old who wanted to crawl and climb everywhere, and she carried a sleeping newborn in a sling on her chest. We were two Brits in a city that wasn't our own, and we were also writers: myself of fiction, and she of poetry. The way she called herself a poet, with such pride and grace, I felt in awe of her and shame for myself for both culling and concealing my own curiosity in the art form. Many months later, on a walk with our children in their buggies, she talked about getting ready to wean her son and she declared she wouldn't be pureeing any vegetables or fruits for him during naptimes. "Why would I spend my free time doing that when there's poetry to write?" She said with a grin. Although we have lost touch since, these words have often bounced around in my head in the four years since - thank you, Natasha!

And then there was Mary. Mary Oliver. I can't remember the first time I read one of her poems, but I would put money on it being one of her most popular ones, like Wild Geese or The Summer Day. It stopped me in my tracks, I am sure, as many of her poems do whether it's just to remind myself to blink while I feel the world find its new order, or to take a breath and go back to the beginning and read the poem again.

I have several of Mary Oliver's poetry collections on my bookshelf and on my bedside table and they belong to a small group of books that I call Powerful Closed Books. What I mean by that is that their power emanates through their closed covers. I have complete trust in the words they contain, but sometimes, depending on my mood, to open them and read a page or two would be too much. They are the mirrors you sometimes don't want to look into, not because you will see things you don't want to see, but because you will *feel* things you're not sure you want or are ready to...

Because on other days, opening up and reading these Powerful Closed Books can feel like the most important message from the universe, one that says in a million different but beautiful ways: You are not alone.

It was exactly this feeling and this message that ultimately attracted me to or rather trapped me into my love affair with poetry in my mid-30s.

After becoming a mother for the first time, I experienced post-natal depression and post-natal anxiety. The former was an old, annoying friend and I got relatively comfy with her quite quickly, reluctantly riding out the lowest of the lows by crying in the burning hot showers I took as often as I could, wearing my baggiest tracksuits, and trying in vain to perk myself up with unhealthy amounts of sugar and caffeine.

But anxiety was a different kind of beast and she waltzed in unannounced whenever she felt like it, with her over-powering physicality and her unpredictable irrationality. She was a demon I had no experience managing and so I didn't see her for what she was until somebody else did - a psychiatrist, no less - in other words the last in a long chain of medical professionals I had sought help from.

Anxiety made me feel too much, and she made me feel different things all the time, or consecutively so quickly I would feel totally out of control. Then she began to attack what little precious new parent sleep I was having, and left me with chronic insomnia, a playground for the darkest of intrusive thoughts. This was when I started to focus not on feeling better, but on just not feeling at all.

Numbness was my goal, and I did everything I could to obtain it, helped greatly by being the parent of an over-active, often grumpy young baby who never slept for more than 45 minutes. (Yes, even at night.) I stopped writing my fiction, I stopped reading books, I wouldn't watch TV shows unless they were predictable or offensively average. Most telling of all, I stopped listening to music and my body forgot to dance; my mouth didn't sing anymore.

Of course, none of it helped. Not really. It only helped me lose myself further when I was already fighting to find out who I was now that my body and my mind had been utterly transformed into a new over-bearing, inescapable identity; that of being a mother.

Never did I expect to lose so much from creating new life.

I am hesitant to compare becoming a mother with a death or dying, but I know with solid certainty that when I did have my first child, I experienced a great amount of grief. I will save the ins and outs of why I think this for another day, but anybody who has ever experienced grief will know that there is no way out of it other than directly through, and with it. You cannot dodge the things that grief wants you to feel, not without suffering the consequences, and seeing as my default setting is usually Feel All The Things, my mission for numbness was doomed and never got very far. All it did do was take away many of brightest lights in my life, and so darkness closed in even more suffocating than before.

Throughout this I found myself writing a weekly motherhood diary on my blog for my son's first year. Pregnant Me had decided to do it in order to document this new experience and all the things I would feel - little did she know! - but Post-Partum Me clung to it like it was a lifeboat out of a stormy shipwreck. In some ways it was; if I was still writing something, and about this experience I was feeling so confused and conflicted about, then I felt like I had some element of control over it. Furthermore, it was a frayed thread of cotton connecting me to one of the most important identities I was so desperately trying to hold on to; writer.

At one of the therapy sessions I had with my first therapist (yes, there were a few!) she suggested I write down what I was feeling. I told her about the Motherhood Diary on my blog which she responded to with a nod and a kind smile, before saying; "No, you should write how you *really* feel. Get the anger, the sadness, and the guilt out of you and onto the page. Nobody has to read it but you."

"Nobody has to read it but you."

This concept felt so radical and revelatory that despite myself, I saw a small glimmer of hope in it.

It's something of a paradoxical confession to say that as a freelance writer, blogger and author of fiction I hadn't consciously entertained the benefit of writing if "nobody has to read it". Professionally, I'd fallen into a trap of only really writing for profit or performance, but as an author I had always been writing as if "nobody has to read it", because I have several drafts of stories that will hopefully never see the light of day. I just hadn't fully acknowledged or celebrated the importance of this.

But as is often a problem for us women, it is not until we are expressly given permission to do something that we realise we were waiting and holding ourselves back.

And so I started to write in those hours I couldn't sleep, my brain so foggy sometimes, weeks later, I would read back the notes I typed on my phone and assume my son had grabbed hold of the device, before seeing the time stamp. But other times the spew of consciousness and subconsciousness formed something I started to recognise; it was poetry.

Being a writer-for-hire and author, it's hard to shake the habit of looking at language strategically and working what you want to say into the structure or pattern that best delivers it, but because I was writing like "nobody has to read it" I gave myself permission to write my words in whatever way felt right.

This lawless "beta" form of my poetry felt the most powerful and empowering of all, and I started to be more deliberate with it. It should also be said that having had all but a fraction of my writing time swept away in order to care for my baby son, poetry offered me many benefits. It was quick, it was flexible and unrestrictive, and it was all about capturing a feeling, or a thought, or a question, or an impact, or a sensation in just a few lines or paragraphs.

Yes, I had come to see that poetry was everything I thought it wasn't.

And as poetry became a pathway for me to start feeling more again, the gift of both giving myself permission to feel again, and permission to process those feelings into poetry, was almost the last push Anxiety needed to pack her bags and leave for good, or at least for a hotel down the road where she only bothers me occasionally on those nights insomnia is back in town. But she is no longer a permanent bedfellow. She is no longer my mistress or master, and in many ways I have poetry to thank for that. Poetry, and the anti-anxiety medication I began to take at night to help me sleep because sadly, it's my experience that no human can live on poems alone.

I think when an art form accompanies you on a journey like this, it is almost impossible to not fall in love with it in a way that you want to share it with others. When you can demonstrate the power of art in your journey, and specifically in your healing and recovery, you want to offer up that opportunity to others. You also want to explore it further. To see where it can take you.

In 2017, just before my son turned two, I did just that by setting myself the challenge of writing 100 poems in 100 days for the online creativity challenge, #the100dayproject. I succeeded in that challenge and most of the poems you read here originate from those 100 days as spring moved into summer three years ago. As you can expect from writing on demand for 100 days in a row, all the while working, parenting, and navigating life's other demands, not all the poems were good, and many were outright awful. Fortunately for us all, I have saved you from the worst ones!

Then there were the poems that came afterwards. They have been included in this collection too because this is their home. Much more than after-thoughts they were the offspring of my mind which through the challenge had become so invested in and focused on certain themes, or rather, certain phases in my life, there was no way the poems would stop coming after 100 days.

There was lust, love, and loss. **Lover.** An era of around ten or fifteen years in my early adulthood. I thought about those years a lot as a new mother and a new poet because they seemed so far away from where I was. Those were the years I danced and sang the most. Those were the years I fell in love with so many people, not just romantic lovers, but friends and strangers, over and over again, delicious nights of fun and free-thinking, followed by the pain of hangovers and heartbreak. And yes, they were also the years I met my life-partner and fell in love with him, an experience that also didn't roll out how I expected. I wanted to write about all of this, even if it was so many years later. Lucky that I did, because it was in writing this with the great benefit of hindsight that I can see I also fell in love with myself, my sexuality, and my womanhood during this Lover stage of life, even if I didn't know it at the time.

Mother. The act of becoming a mother, and all the experiences and struggles that brought to me, was what brought me to poetry, or rather what poetry brought out of me. And it wasn't all bad, hard or sad. Because aside from anxiety and depression, and the grief of losing who I had been, there was also the intensity of my love for my firstborn, and then second son, the connections I made with other mothers, the impact of it on my relationships, and the precious fragility of the many joys we share as a family. To capture all of this in poems is a treasure I can't quite give full credit to with words, but I feel it in my bones, my heart, and my gut, so I know that it is very real and very special.

And then there was everything else. All the other things I still was. All the other things I still am.

All the other things I will still be. **Other.** These Others matter too. In fact, their mattering too has been the saving of me (again and again) during my worst moments of depression and anxiety, and crucial in my making my own version of motherhood a positive experience. It is only right that they are the final chapter, because while identities, roles, and labels do define us, rightly or wrongly, they should never be constricting or limiting. They should never put us in boxes or clip our wings. They should never be finite. You can always be, do, see, and feel more. And all being well, so you will.

I am 38 now and I love poetry. And yes, I'm still a Lover. I will always be a Mother too, but I cannot and will not quantify what Other I am because I hope it is ever-changing and never-ending.

Proof of that is this book, because as well as Lover, Mother and Other, I am also now, very proudly, a Poet.

Frances M. Thompson, November 2020

LOVER

You left me

"You left me, sweet, two legacies,—

A legacy of love

A Heavenly Father would content,

Had He the offer of;

You left me boundaries of pain

Capacious as the sea,

Between eternity and time,

Your consciousness and me."

Emily Dickinson

Watching

I see your chest rise.
I see your chest fall.
Your inner workings are silent
But your breath says it all.

I sit and I watch,
I wait and I wait.
For I am still young enough
To tease Mistress Fate.

I twitch my feet forward,
I reach for my phone.
My love, I'm going now,
Watching you hurts my bones.

I walk and I walk,
I shake my head twice.
I should have said bye.
I should have said hi.

Your Sweet, Sweet Music

You have to make me feel more
Than the wandering low notes
Plucked from the body
Of a deep double bass.

You have to make me shiver
More than the crescendo of
A string quartet, surrendering
To their own blissful triumph.

You have to make me feel fuller
Than the sound of a drummer
Hammering their heart out,
Losing their limbs to rhythm.

You have to make me want to dance
Like I'm the only one who can
Hear, see, touch and feel,
Your sweet, sweet music.

A Dating Mantra

I'm not playing hard to get.
I'm playing hard to win.
Because
I
Am
A
Prize.

My Love Song

It was never about
Taking you,
Owning you,
Plunging into you and
Making you mine.

It was about
Nestling my nose
Into the valley of
Your collar bone,
And letting my chin
Hear how strong,
Feel how soft,
Your heart beats.

18-30

I've had summers where I've fallen in love
With ten men and three women.
Two on the same day,
Seven in the same week,
As I danced on a beach
And swam naked in the sea,
And kissed and held and squeezed,
While arching my chin up and
Silently urging the sun to
Stay exactly where it was.
That gentle hum of pink,
The noiseless, warm air,
That peachy promise of
Another perfect day.

Delicate

I feel you
Searching
My inside
Seams and
Unfinished
Hems.

Looking for
The label
With care
Instructions
For my lonely
Heart.

Neon (A Haiku)

You make me feel like
Fifty shades of neon pink
Blue, yellow, and green.

Sweet Like Chocolate

Sometimes I taste chocolate without putting it on my tongue.
Sometimes I feel kissed while alone in the shower.
Sometimes I wake from a fitful sleep full of new life.
Sometimes I dance to a song nobody can hear, not even my ears.
Sometimes I know I don't need anything but me. Just me.
Today is not one of those days.
Today I want the music, the sleep, the kisses, and all the chocolate.
Because I also know I am worthy of good company.

I Don't Know You But...

There is something about you
That makes me want to
Climb up on my chair,
Mount the table,
Crawl my way over,
And read poetry to you.

Her Smiles

I love the way
Her back smiles
In seven places
As she sits up
After lying down
With me.

VI - III

Crack up.
Let some love in.

Let Your Miracle Grow (for B&C)

Days end,
Credits roll,
Doors close,
But
Love…
If you feed it,
Love just grows and grows and grows and grows and
grows and grows and grows.

Laughter (A Haiku)

Laughter is the sound
Love makes as it goes from one
Heart to another.

Masks

Watch her take her make-up off.
Follow the gliding of her hand,
The unmasking of her truth which
Blemishes, freckles, and wrinkles.

See the colours she tries to hide,
The dips and dulls, blues and reds.
Marvel at her skin's ability to be
Soft and smooth here, a little dry there.

Watch where she looks in the mirror.
Why is it at the peaks and plateaus
She spends so long covering up?
Why not the ones she loves most?

And as she finishes, tissues in the bin,
Ask her if you can touch her new
Nakedness. If yes, graze your fingertips
Over her cheeks, her chin, her jaw.

Watch her as you stroke the arch of
Her eyebrow, and tease at her hairline.
Lose your fingers in her curls and make
Her eyelashes dance with your breath.

See another mask is lifted. The one

That assumes she looks better with
A painted face full of half-truths or
Half lies. Watch it disappear...

That mask you were wearing when you first met her.

Like Cheese Sauce

Let it slow and thicken;
Your breath,
The time,
Our love.

Burn, Baby, Burn

There was fire once,
A long time ago.
The spark has gone now
And cannot be re-lit.

But we are not ashes.
We are embers that
Burn bright, glow slow, and
Offer a little light, a lot of love.

Who's to say when the red
Shall turn amber, then
Black? Not me. I want more.
So until then, please stay,

And keep me warm.

One Thing's for Sure

Well, one thing's for sure,
I said, wine glass in hand,
Lip-glossed cigarette tap-tapped.

In ten years or more, when I'm middle-aged and fat,
with kids running around everywhere, and a husband
who loves me just as I am, and a beautiful big house
that is always a mess, and I am so utterly happy with
it all…

I won't even remember his name, let alone how good
he looked underneath me, or how we watched the
sun go down while my legs were still shaking from
his loving.

You know what I mean?
I said, wine glass topped up,
Cigarette sucked and stubbed out.

It definitely won't keep me up at night then, I can tell
you.

I said,
But I guess I was lying.

Poetry is All Around

Everyone's a poet
When they say
I love you.

Us

Sparks fly

Out of
Faulty plug
Sockets.

Butterflies swirl

Around flowers
Only to die
A day later.

Magic happens

When hands
Move quicker
Than the eye.

You and me,

We choose to be
Together.
And that is that.
Until it isn't.

Forever and Ever

I think I'm falling in love with you
Didn't take the bins out and it's your turn to
Make me scream your name so loud I
Lost my keys. Where did you put them? Please
Never stop kissing me. Promise me, that you'll
Get up with them, I did it yesterday and I'm so
Ready to stay like this with you forever and ever and
ever.

VI - I

Come at me,
Like you care.

Hung Up

After putting down the phone
I cried, of course. In a pile
On the floor, chest heaving,
Body groaning, mouth moaning.

But very quickly I had a thought,
About something that would help.
It was clear and true and made
Strange, solid, soothing sense.

I should pick up the phone and
Call you to tell you all about this
Thing that had just happened to
Me, and the hot, hot pain I was in.

You would listen. You would care.
You would want to know
All about how very hard
You had broken my heart.

Magic

He was a magician.
He made me fly so very high.
And then he vanished.

Right Wrong Love

They fell in love at exactly the right wrong time.
Or was it the wrong right time?
Either way it felt right but they knew it was wrong.
And when they parted, they knew it was right to feel
all wrong, for oh, so very long.

VI - V

You're my solace,
But no solution.

Dandelion Kisses

Every time you kiss me, I think
About the pollen of a dandelion
Being blown away
Breath by breath,
Push by push,
Until there is nothing left.

Seasons

I was a leaf in autumn,
Fiery, ever-changing, and ready to fall.

You were the blossom of spring,
Soft, surprising, and so very welcome.

Of course, I fell for you.
Of course, you weren't soft at all.

Together we faded away...
A few weeks and it was done.

Now I'm a tree in winter,
Bare, cold, and immovable.

And you are a summer flower,
Full of sweet nectar and promise.

We live on opposite sides of time.
It's where we belong.

But what do you think people want
In the hot heat of summer?

And where do you think people go
When the winter winds blow too strong?

In other words, I will always want you.
And you will always want me to want you too.

Oh (A Haiku)

It's hard to accept
That, like all you want for
Life, love is a phase.

Farewell Sunbeam

You are a sunbeam
Dancing on the surface
Of the dark, deep water
I find myself drowning in.

Mills & Boom

She read stories about pirate kings and narrow-waisted women who longed for a man to light them up from the inside out.

He read the newspaper's sport pages, the small print on receipts, and a note from his wife saying goodbye.

Over

The details don't matter. All that
Matters is that it's
Over.

That sweet song we sang together
For the fullest year of
My life.

Already I have exhaled a million
Heartbroken sighs, and each one
Confirms

My new reality of thinking about
You more than I ever did
Before.

Leaving

And in those first one hundred steps
Away from you,
A thousand times I thought about
Going back.

Under the Covers

You always have preferred cover versions,
Songs not sung by those who wrote them.
Songs that never sound how they should.
Songs that we all know the words to,
But they come out a little differently.
I tell myself that's why you prefer
Her love to mine.
She sings the same tune, just a little differently.
But I am the original.
I will always be the original.

Hold On

Don't you know
All those things he said
That made you feel so
Loved.

They're all still true.
Them and a million more.
All true. Even if he is
Not.

Conquered

They walked with the purpose of a mountain
Climber, straight up the steep and jagged edge
Of my fragile heart. I let them conquer
Me, and they stabbed a pole's sharp end
In deep.

Now a frayed flag flaps madly in the wind,
Abandoned and alone.
It's like nobody was ever there…

Living (Leaving) Language (A Haiku)

Like a circumflex
Something still remained, but the
Real you was long gone.

What Harm

You seemed no worse than wet crumbs at the bottom
of my teacup,
A soggy sight I didn't want to taste on my tongue.
I let you hold my hand.
What harm would that do?
But even my fingers still tingle
With the damage you have done.

Facelook

I still type your name
And click Search.
Just to check you're still there,
Somewhere.

My Many Loves

His love was a soaring kind,
Like a kite in high winds,
The string only so strong.

Her love was a gentle touch
I almost didn't notice,
But once I did, I craved too much.

Their love was the fleeting kind.
Limbs merge and mesh and my mind
Misplaces names, moles, tattoos.

Your love is the stillest water,
I float slowly, lazily along,
Oblivious most of the time.

And my love? I wish I knew
What my love was like. I wish
I could ask him and her and them.

And you.

Shades of Love (A Haiku)

No colour has more
Shades than green, apart from love.
Love. Love has the most.

To Those Who Left Me...

I'm still here.
I am still love.
I am still.
LOVE.

MOTHER

"You thought you know me,

But I did know you,

You thought you were watching me,

But I did hold you securely in my sight,

Recording every moment,

Memorizing your smiles, tracing your frowns.

In your absence

I rehearsed you,

The way you had of singing

On a breeze,

While a sob lay

At the root of your song."

Maya Angelou, from Mother, A Cradle to

Hold Me

My Rose

Your skin,
Like rose petals,
So soft,
I have to look,
To check that
I am really touching you,
Holding you.
And I am.
I am,
I am.
I am
A mother now.
My little rose,
I am your mother.

Twice

Every day now
The sun rises twice.
Once
When you reach for me,
Twice
When daylight comes.

Forever Pregnant

While you live outside me now,
I am still pregnant,
With worry,
With hope,
With fear,
With all the love I'm yet to give you.
It's the fullest and the heaviest I've ever been.

VI - VII

For you, darling,
Nothing but sunshine.

Before the Baby Comes

In a bag you must pack
Nappies, bottles, and pants
That are so big and grey
They will blackout the sun.

Your freezer you must fill
With meals you may not
Want to eat one day, but will
Gorge your tired heart on the next.

At home you must get
A cot, a basket, a swinging
Chair. A pram, a carrier, and
20 muslin cloths for your tears.

Tell your friends to ditch the
Flowers for wine, swap gifts for
The washing up, and to ignore
You when you say you're fine.

In your bag you must pack
A list of 100 things you love to
Do, and make, and be, because
You will forget. You will forget.

A Mother's Work

However it happens,
A woman must hurt
A little or a lot,
And then heal
A little or a lot,
To become a mother.

The Birth of a Mother

No matter the story.
No matter what happened.
No matter how good it was.
No matter how bad it was.
No matter what took place before.
No matter what came after.
No matter how many times it happens again.
No matter if it never happens again.
There is no getting over the first time a human births
a child,
The first time a human births a mother.

She wears this honour and this burden every day
thereafter,
Like her most precious jewellery,
Like a tattoo she sometimes regrets,
Like a scar on her body only she can see.
A scar she sometimes struggles to love,
But still,
She finds comfort in remembering it, touching it,
knowing it.
Owning it.

I love you so so so so much I
Could,
Would,
And just
Did
Burst
Open
For
You.

- **Notes on Childbirth**

Message in a Bottle

What they will tell you
Loud and clear, with
Their flowers and wide smiles
And maybe moistened eyes,

Is that you are blessed
And lucky, and every
Moment is to be cherished
Before time takes it away.

What some will tell you
In a whisper, or in a
Letter, written hurriedly
On tear-stained paper,

Is that it may well be
The hardest thing you do
That there will be moments
Of hate and pain and regret,

And shame and guilt and
What did you do? Why
Did you give yourself the job
Of carrying this around forever?

This new, big, cumbersome love of yours.

But what nobody will tell you but me,
And I am you, and you are me
Is that it will be both.
It will be all this. And so much more.

How are YOU?

He is safe.
He is warm.
He is fed.
He is loved.
He is happy.
He is not alone.

Now, how about you?

(Un)Plugged

In those torturous hours
When the incessant cries
Pierce through your ribs
And into your heart,
Remember how much,
You wanted them
To cry that first cry.
How much you
Wanted to hear
Their big, loud life.
Remember that,
Inhale that.
Exhale that

Now go and find some earplugs.

Look at My Belly

I see you
Looking at my Belly.
Its sag,
Its lag,
It's a bag
Of the best of me.
The part of me
That cuddles my food,
And oh, yes,
Made and housed some humans too.

Look at my Belly
And judge
Me for the
Cake I ate.
The runs I
Didn't make,
The muscles I
Don't use and
The sit-ups I
Ditch for sit-downs on my glorious bum.

I do it too,
Of course.
I look,
I stare,

I judge,
And compare.
Fake comfort
In bigger Bellies,
Darker stripes,
Saggier, more magical skin than mine.

So I say,
Do it, friends,
And foe.
Look at my Belly.
Watch it stick around
Long after my
Babies are grown
And my
Food gone.
And watch me loving my big soft Belly.

Not for
The babies
Not for
The food,
But because
It is My Belly
My Jelly
My Body
My Spaceship
For as long as I am on this world.

PPD

If you chopped my brain in two,
I'm sure you would find a lot of
The colour and the glitter and the sparkle
Missing.

It would be a monochrome mess,
Grey blobs where sparks should fly,
And muffled groaning where neurons should sing
And dance.

It would explain a lot. It would maybe
Even start to make sense, albeit a silent
Sad revelation, that wouldn't bring back
The light.

But I do not want you to chop my brain in two.
I want it to be whole, and ready for the colour,
The glitter, the sparkle. To come back
As soon as it can.

Because it will. One day, one day. It will
And we will be ready for the singing and dancing
Oh yes, we will, my neurons, my baby
And me.

You Didn't

You didn't feel your body split open and never go back together the same way.
You didn't suffer the stabbing pain of being sucked and hardened and tugged for hours on end.
You didn't push yourself up on arms that were shaking and haul your bleeding body out of bed.
You didn't strap him to your chest and carry him everywhere, anywhere, just so he'd calm.
You didn't bleed for three weeks and worry about the Earth falling out of you five times a day.
You didn't crave the most boring, mundane comforts because you still had them.
You didn't feel your insides curdle when the cries came despite giving your all to that little life.
You didn't wonder when it was that your sense of humour was sucked out of you.
You didn't lie awake when the whole world slept, counting the ways it was all too much.
You didn't look skywards when you felt sure something was going to fall on him and end it all.
You didn't force the relief you felt at this possible tragedy down, down, down into the darkest depths of you.
You didn't.
You didn't.

But I did.

Every Day

Every day that I feel full to bursting
With love, pride, joy, and love,
I sit down and drink tea with
The thought that becoming
Empty beyond compare
Is just a breath away.

My Balloon Heart

You stick animals on my hand
And pins in my balloon heart.

They must stay there forever
Because everyone knows what

Happens when you pull a pin
Out of a full balloon.

Elastic

There was no pinging.
I didn't snap back
Into the body
Or the person
I was before.

I must be elastic
Because I
Stretched far
Beyond where
I thought I
Could,
Should,
Would,
Ever go.

But unlike a rubber band,
I haven't let go.
I haven't felt the pull
Back.
No pinging.
No tightening.
No undoing.
Just stretching.

If anything,

I stretch on.
Forever stretching.
Forever bending.
Forever breaking a bit.
But not completely.

May I always stretch,
May I always stay elastic
For you.   (And for me too.)

Heartbeat

To watch the one you love most fall asleep
Is to believe all is well in the world
If only for a heartbeat.

On Motherhood

I find it all hard.
All of it.

Apart from loving you.
That bit I can do.

Blindfolded, gagged, and trapped in a rocket hurtling
to the moon, that bit I'd still be able to do.

A Mother's Love

A mother's love is like the sun.
You cannot look directly at it or get too close.
For to examine it so thoroughly
Would make you wonder
Why something so powerful
Could ever be laid on the shoulders of a human being.
But like the sun, a mother's love is more
Necessary that we'll ever know.
And like the sun, this mother's love will keep on
burning, hurting, and healing,
In almost equal measure.

Dear Toddler

The rumbling of your sleeping breath
Is a song I could listen to forever.
The fullness of your resting cheeks
Is innocence in its fleshiest form.

The twitching fingers of your fists
Hold more potential than I can measure.
The scoop of your dainty eyelashes
Asks to be grazed with a kiss…

But I don't lean in, I don't disturb.
I close the door and drink my wine.
For while you are the most beautiful thing in sleep,
You are a challenging little love awake.

So I close my eyes, stretch out my fingers,
And take rumbling breaths of my own,
Drawing in strength for another day
With my most beautiful, challenging love.

Today

A wild wind waltzes in and
My hair tangles and ties
In a thousand tiny knots.
But I won't worry about them
Nor the dirt under
My fingernails, or the
Shape of my eyebrows
With their supporting hairs
Rising up out of place.
Because today everything else
Was perfectly positioned.
Because today we were together.

VI - VIII

You are
One million
Brilliant tomorrows.

A Love that Carves...

Sometimes I feel like the love I give you carves its
own way out of me.
A spoon's dull edge scraping along the very pit of me.
But I am never hollow.
Never.

My Eyes

He has my eyes.
But of course, he doesn't.
His eyes are his eyes,
And they see things
That my own do not,
Nor ever could.

I've tried to see what
He sees. To watch and
Learn through his eyes,
And ears, and far reaching hands.
But it's not possible.

For they may be the same shape,
Size and chestnut brown,
But they are his eyes and
They see only what he sees,
Which is fine with me.

Because my eyes still see
The most beautiful of things.
Like him seeing with his eyes.
And him hearing with his ears.
And his hands,
Reaching for me.

The Softest Skin I Have Ever Known

For some, it's your toes
Your full, full cheeks,
Or the rolls gathered
On all of your limbs.

But for me, it's your neck.
So strong from day one,
It is what connects your
Busy mind and busy body.

In that curve I seek and
I sniff. I kiss. Eyes closed.
Under your chin I find
The softest skin I have ever known.

I urge your neck to grow stronger
Every day. May it always
Help you face the world
With a smile tilted to the sky.

A Little List

Love.
Imagination.
Curiosity.

These are the things I hope you always have.

Some days, it's homemade muffins for breakfast.
Some days, it's pushing a swing 100 times in the rain.
Some days, it's catching vomit in your hands.
Some days, it's handing over the biscuit you craved all morning.
Some days, it's scraping playdough out of the carpet.
Some days, it's sobbing as you fold away baby clothes.
Some days, it's singing Old MacDonald at the top of your lungs.
Some days, it's sitting in the darkness on their floor until a butt cheek goes numb.
And some days, it's simply not running for the hills as they call your name so loud it burns your bones.

- How to Be a Good Mother

Bone Deep

It is truly bone deep.
Piercing through my fascia,
Penetrating the marrow,
Weighing down my every move.
Bone, bone, bone deep.
The exhaustion,
And the love.

-

Whispers

I do not tiptoe
Into your room
To tuck you in
Or kiss your brow.

I do not tiptoe
Into your room
To tell you
You are the best thing that ever happened to me.

I tip-toe into
Your room to
Just watch and
Feel whatever I feel.

I tip-toe into
Your room to
Tell you that
You are the best thing that is happening to me.

Keep happening to me.
Keep happening to me.
Keep happening to me.

Just You Wait

I don't think there's anyone who could love you more
than I do now.
Hold up, lady. Said a big knowing voice. Yes, there is.
Who? I asked.
You tomorrow.

Stroke

Don't stop.
Keep stroking your stomach
Because even though they
Are not there anymore
You are still here.

OTHER

I went down to the river,

I set down on the bank.

I tried to think but couldn't,

So I jumped in and sank.

I came up once and hollered!

I came up twice and cried!

If that water hadn't a-been so cold

I might've sunk and died.

Langston Hughes, from Life is Fine

Missing Mary

We should have put gloves on
This morning. It was cool enough
And the grass was grey and crisp,
Kissed with the year's first frost.

I think of you as I stand and watch
My son run around the park,
Giggling and toddling and turning
Back, just to grin at me, eyes bright.

I'm so glad you met him I
Think dreamily to myself with a
Slow smile until I realise
No. You didn't. You were

Already. A noise escapes my
Lips. It comes from my lungs,
Or gut, or wherever it is that I
Feel the full weight of things.

No. You met my eldest but no,
Not this one. He was growing and
Kicking inside me as I sang
The hymns at your funeral and

The sadness of that feels sharp

Enough to break my heart apart,
But it doesn't. So. I take another
Deep breath and look up to

See my son picking himself up too.
You'd love this cool fresh air,
I think as I watch my boy run
Back to me, his cold hands held out

Pink and wet because the frost
Is dew now. Autumn is here,
Our dance before winter, and
We should have put gloves on.

This morning.

Alive

Your life
Pulses outside
Of flat-
Shaped things
And moving
Images that
You stare
At. Inanimate.

Your life,
Your love,
Burns brightest
In moments
Shared and
Words heard
And yes,
In words

Spoken. But
More in
Words heard.
Slowly, carefully,
Lovingly heard.
For then
You show you
Care. Then

You show
You are
There. Here.
Everywhere.
And
You
Are

Alive.

Two-wheeled Love (for Amsterdam)

It shakes my bones and creates breeze wherever I go.
It is the closest thing to flying I will ever know.
For every hill climbed there's a promise to come.
Of soaring freer and faster than I could ever run.
Even clanking, I feel as graceful as a swan.
Even wobbling, I decide my destination.
Even rattling, I roll on my rusty old version
Of the world's greatest invention.

Cocoon

How can you expect us not to believe in magic when one of the first true stories we are told is that of the caterpillar and the butterfly?

Home

Thank you, walls for holding up the roof that shelters those I love.
Thank you, windows for keeping the rain out but letting the light in.
Thank you, door for opening when I need you to, and staying closed when I don't.
Thank you, stairs for taking me to the place I sleep and leading me down to a new day.
Thank you, foundations for staying strong and bearing the weight of us.
Thank you, floors for letting us walk, dance, run, lie, sit and live all over you.
Thank you, home, for being where we breathe slower and easier and together.
Thank you, Home, for being ours.

Murmuration

Above me they soar in listless shapes.
Led by one, I'll never know which,
They dance the same way, together.

Every evening they celebrate the day
That is done, and the night yet to come.
The hours of rest we have all earned.

But I have seen them in the morning too
Those swirling black clouds above
That cast a spell and leave me torn.

Torn between wanting to join them...
And wanting to stay forever
Flightless and grounded.

For to join them would mean losing
The joy of watching, watching, watching.

A Spring of Faith

I've been walking around
Thinking, wondering
Why we call spring
Life's new beginning?

These beautiful blooms,
The colours winter forgot,
Aren't they in reality
A sweet prelude to rot?

The spreading of petals
Like a stretch of the arms,
Says my work here,
It's done. It's done.

The sadness of this
Slows my thoughts and
Closes my eyes. It pulls
At my mouth, and my mind.

But didn't you notice?
The flowers whisper (to me),
That we were at our finest
Just before we died.

Remember, My Darlings

Remember, my darling,
Wounds itch when they heal.
Roses will always have thorns.
And water saves lives but it can
Also suck them under.

Remember, my darling,
Some weeds look like flowers.
Some flowers look like weeds.
Trees give us the air we breathe,
And yet we cut them down.

Remember, my darling,
Wasps and bees sting, but only bees
Make honey. We need the sea, but the sea
Will never need us. And doors,
They open as well as close.

Remember, my darling,
Being alone is not the same as being lonely.
Your love is free, until you put a price on it.
And bravery doesn't defeat fear.
It keeps it company.

Remember, my darling, please remember.

We speak different languages, wear different clothes, have different bodies, love different bodies, and every morning we stretch out into skin that is seven billion and a half different colours.

But we all bleed, and we all bleed red.

VI – IIII

All our tears
Taste the same.

The Strangeness of Kindness

All this noise
About letting go, releasing, setting things free.
Well, what about
Letting in, welcoming, giving things a home.
Like empathy,
Trust,
Respect,
Compassion,
Kindness,
Love.
A stranger, or two?

Just Before Dusk

The blossom dances its last
As it skips through the air.
Heading here, there or nowhere,
It doesn't seem to care.

The jet streams cross the sky
On their pre-ordained routes.
As they slice into the blue,
I urge just one to loop-the-loop.

The birds' chirping maddens;
They are tired like me.
May they find their nests safely;
That's where I long to be.

Watching the day slowly end,
The colours beginning to fade,
My breath comes back to me,
And tomorrow is another day.

Apricity

He thought that the sun
Always meant warmth.
He learned the hard way
That the sun could also shine
On the coldest of winter days.

But you had to admire him,
That bare skin turning pink
As he walked into a cruel cold,
The kind that is invisible
But tangible all over.

Just hanging there in the air,
Waiting to burn a young man's
Fingertips, toes, and dreams.
Naked, he learned that the sun
Didn't always offer warmth.

In love, he learned that you
Could be lying next to the hottest
Star in the universe, bask in her
Warmth and beauty, and still
Freeze.

Style

Ladies,
They're wrong.
You can have too many
Handbags, shoes, and
Little black dresses.
What you can't have too many of
Are books, friends, and memories
That make your heart sing.

Repeat (A Haiku)

Repeat after me.
A woman does not need a
King to be a Queen.

Wrinkles

Love your wrinkles
They are a legacy built by your
Smiles.

10

There was a time,
A decade or so ago,
When one morning,
As the birds sang outside
And the sun warmed up the Earth,
I pulled on a pair of size 10 jeans
And they held my body tighter than any man could.
A little loving,
A little suffocating.
I can only vaguely remember when that was.
I can only vagulely remember what that felt like.
I certainly don't remember the birds or the sun or if I
smiled at my long, hard, unhappy year of
achievement in the mirror.
All this leads me to conclude
Those jeans,
That size 10 body of mine,
It really wasn't that great.
Not like the sun shining,
Not like the birds singing,
Not like the loving that holds me now.

(Un)Friends

Even if I do not write on your wall
I am thinking of you.

Saved

I didn't delete your number.
It's still there on my phone.
Nor did I delete the memories
Of a friendship I thought would never end…

Oh, how I hope you're well.

How I Feel About Time

The days pass me by
Like clouds in the sky.
Indistinguishable shapes,
Each one has a fate.

I look back far too much,
The hurt and anger, I touch.
How I wish I'd walked outside
When it was sunny and bright.

The past had more substance
Than the future or present.
Memories gave me relief,
Even if it was bittersweet.

So I search for the energy
To treasure each and every
Moment I'm given,

Given,

Given,

But I just don't have it in me.

I prefer my time to be fluid,

Floating, fading, rarely lucid.
Like me, who will always be
A woman changing,
Incessantly.

Dear Body

Dear Body,

Please know that I am truly sorry, forever grateful, and everything in between.

You are my best friend,

Love,
Me.

Let Us Pray

Let us learn
To shed our
Most negative
Of thoughts,
Like the skin cells
And dead hairs
We no longer need.

?

The sunlight that wakes me.
The hot water that washes me.
The tea that soothes me.
The food that fuels me.
The clothes that cover me.
The shoes that carry me.
The steps I take to work.
The steps I take back home.
The sky that fades from blue to black.
The clouds that decorate it.
The moon that also rises.
The stars that burn above.
The pillow I lay my head on.
The darkness I hope to sleep in.
I ask all of these things what I should do,
They reply again and again and again.
But they never give me an answer.

VI - X

Sometimes
Luck has
H o l e s
In it.

Upside Down

Why is it, that in public, we feel no fear in laughing
with all our might?
But we drown in a swallowing shame when we cry
our soul out in front of another?

Blurry

I looked to my left and saw thick rain crisscrossing its way to the ground.

I turned my head to the right and saw sunshine warming all the dry air in between the clouds and the earth.

I searched with my eyes, trying to define the exact line where the rain met the sun, searching for a rainbow.

Forever searching for a rainbow.

But I couldn't find it.
Only a blurred line of rain and sun.
Only a blurred line.

Forever blurred lines.

Places

The breast of my mother.
The shoulder of my father.
The carpet of my brother's room.
The duvet of my sister's bed.
Into ever-changing pillowcases
Someone else chose, until I did.

The tiled floor in the toilets of
My first, second, third school.
The corner of a crowded dancefloor
In cities up and down the country.
In Jake's house, and Robert's too,
Alone in their bathrooms.

My back against a wall outside
The office of my first boss, my
Second boss, but not the third.
As the organ played in churches
Announcing new loves or old lives.
In the sickly sterile air of a hospital ward.

In the warped mirror of a changing room.
On a bike, a bus, a train, a plane.
In the arms of friends, real and fake.
On the silky soft hair of my firstborn
As he riled and wriggled in my arms.

Against the one who said he'd never leave.

Into nothing and no-one, again and again.

These are all the places I have cried.
So far…

Beautiful Wild

When you break in two
You create space
For beautiful wild
Things to grow.

VI - II

Learning to swim,
In my tears.

VI - IX

Breathe in
Out
And
T h r o u g h   it.

Relax, young one.
Not every day is for the winning.
That doesn't mean you've lost or are lacking.
It just means good things can be small as well as big.

- **A Letter to My Younger Self.**

Let the Winds Come

Trees do not shiver.
They shake or sway.
They bend in a breeze.
No more will I shiver,
Tremble or shudder.
I will shake, sway and bend, and
Let the winds rush through and
Past me.

Winter is Going

It's April.
The sun is shining.
The blossom is sneezing open.
The sky is a new shade of blue.
It all makes me exhale deeply because,
Phew,
Looks like we finally made it through.

Heart to Heart

The heart   it knows,
And the heart, it will wait,
Until the heart welcomes,
What it always knew
To be your
Truth:
You.

What's Mine is Mine

I take my time
Because
Contrary to
Everything
Cap
It
All
Ism
Taught me,
My time,
It is mine to take.

Gone

Let them go.
There's nothing to be gained
From someone who wants to leave you.

Shine

Your light
Does not exist
To brighten others' darkness.
Your light exists,
To brighten your own.

Oh, Nina

Birds flying high,
They don't know how I feel.
But you, Nina,
Sometimes I really believe
That you do.

When You Walk In A Room And Don't Know Why You're There, After Trauma, Or Just In Everyday Life

Instead of nagging at yourself
Where was I?

Try smiling instead, and say,
I'm here now.

Lessons

Every year I
Take for granted
The daylight that
Every year I
Hurt for once it
Disappears.

And

Every year I
Fall in love with
The daylight that
Every year I
Dance in once
It returns.

So

Every year we
Learn lessons we
Should already know.

Or

Maybe

Every year we
Learn lessons we
Need to learn
Again.

What I Whisper to the Trees

I want to tell you the same thing
I whisper to the trees:
I have never seen your roots
But I believe in them.

First Aid

In hot, hot showers,
With sugary cups of tea,
Lost in almost good enough hugs,
Tasting your tears,
Taking deep breaths,
You will get through this.

On Crying

What made you think
That crying was
When the pain
Really kicked in?

Didn't they tell you
That crying is
Actually when
Your healing

Begins.

You Will Always Have Them

Find as many as you can
The ones that make the most sense.
Hold them close and play
With them in that busy head of yours.
Think about their peculiar beauty
Before you fall asleep,
And let them visit you in
Your deepest, weirdest dreams.

Wake up the next morning
And smile at the knowledge
You will always have them,
Every single day of
Your bizarre and brilliant life.
As long as you take the time
To know and honour them,
And to write them down.

These words will always love you.
These words. Your words.

We Could Be Heroes

I write.
What's your magic power, superhero?

The Hunt

Most of the time
It's a hunt.
A hunt without a kill.

Each day
I set off,
Determined,
And armed.

I return fruitless
And empty
As my white
Blank page.

But other times
I spot my prey,
I crawl towards it,
I narrow my eyes,
I speak its name,
Type out its skeleton
And hope that the bones have legs…

Hungover

The laughter here smells like the night before.
A haze of giggles born out of the things
He said, she said, they did when they
Were other versions of themselves.

The details are shared as photos and hearsay,
Sobered-up, near forgotten, almost true.
The smiles are full but ache a little, like
Their foreheads, their legs, their livers.

The café's speakers spit out a different song,
One I used to sway my hips to.
Have I forgotten how to dance? How to
Wrap my arms around a stranger's neck and heart?

Now I sit among them, alone, when once
I would lead the pack. I have tea, a clear head,
A notebook, and a pen. I am creating
Just as much drama and fun as any of them.

The Words

Verb
Is the word
For a word
That does something.
But what is the word
For a word
That makes you
Undeniably,
Unassailably,
Irrevocably,
Feel something?

Thank u (A Haiku)

You will always be
The one who taught me what a
Haiku poem is.

Auto-correct

I just wrote a poem
On an app on my phone
As I walked down the street,
A dribble of sweat
Snaking down my back.

In the poem I used the word
Self.
But my phone wanted to write
Self-doubt.

That says more about me than any poem could.

Blocked

Searching for inspiration I listen to songs
From a time when screens were see-through
And belonged only on the front of cars.

I close my eyes and try to think of words
That whisper their way into the soul
Rather than echoing briefly in the ear.

I run through a long, meandering list of things
To write about, but none of them stick.
They slide away like raindrops on a windowpane.

Sometimes it just does not come
Sometimes the search is all I have
Sometimes the search is enough.

For You

Don't you know who I'm writing for?
Don't you see the words are all yours?

Don't you understand, it's your heart
I want to talk to with poems about love and life and
lingering pain.

Don't you feel something when you read my words?
Don't they top you up just a little bit?

Don't they make you stop and sigh?
Don't they make you feel more alive?

Don't you know that I'm doing it all for you?
All of these words, all of the writing, it's for you.

And by you, don't you know I mean me.

Storytime

The best thing a story can do is not make you stop and think.
The best thing a story can do is make you stop. Full stop.

100 Poems

i.
Nestled in between the lines
Words, beats and syllables,
Is something else:
A slow, sweet release.

ii.
I didn't think I had 100 poems in me,
Back then.
But now I know I have 100 poems in me,
Always.

iii.
I am a woman who wrote 100 poems in 100 days.
I am a woman who has 100 stories about how they
came to be.
I am a woman who has less pain than 100 days ago.
I am a woman who has more love in her life thanks to
100 poems.

YOU, Yourself & You

In the beginning
There was **YOU**.

And at the end
There will be **YOU**.

In the middle will
Be many.

And **YOU.**
And **you.**
And you.

Don't forget...
Don't abandon...
Don't lose...

Keep the firmest,
Most loving,
Hold on
YOU.

"Love is old.

Love is new.

Love is all.

Love is you."

The Beatles

Acknowledgements

My thanks, firstly, to those of you who wanted this book three years ago after I originally completed the creative challenge of writing one poem every day for 100 days. Life intervened, specifically in the form of my second child, and getting this work out into the world in this specific form took a backseat. But this also created space for many new poems to make their way into this collection, and I am grateful for that. I have learned many lessons from the delay, and I think it's a better collection now for the additions this time brought, but regardless, thank you for your patience.

Secondly, I'd like to thank my partner and children for filling my days with the one thing I write about most often: love. I love you all, and I dearly love us as a family.

Thirdly, my thanks are indebted to my friend Catherine who has championed my poetry and this book for a long time, indeed for longer than I have. But much more than that she is a champion of me, just as I am, which is worth more to me than any number of poems. Thank you, Cat.

I would also like to thank Nina, who drew illustrations to accompany the poems, and she created the cover artwork too. She also surprised me with an original watercolour painting for one of my poems, and it was one of the happiest surprises of my life. Furthermore, her patience in both dealing with me and waiting for the final book to materialize is one of her many kindnesses and strengths. I am happy to know and work with you, Nina.

And my thanks to you, dear reader, for making it to the end. Although I do hope, in some ways, it also feels like a beginning.

About the Author

Frances M. Thompson is the author of three collections of short stories – Shy Feet, London Eyes, Nine Women – and one suspense novella, The Wait.

Originally from London, UK, Frances now lives in Amsterdam, the Netherlands, with her partner and two young children. She works as a freelance content creator, writer, and as a travel and lifestyle blogger (www.asthebirdfliesblog.com). Frances is currently working on more short stories, poems, and a novel.

Frances, more often known as Frankie, is also the founder and creator of WriteNOW Cards, affirmation cards for writers (@writenowcards on Instagram).

When her kids and writing are being unusually quiet, Frankie likes to spend her time reading, caring for her 100+ houseplants, vintage-shopping, and riding her bike around Amsterdam's canals with her camera.

Other Books by Frances M. Thompson

Shy Feet: Short Stories Inspired by Travel

London Eyes: Short Stories

Nine Women: Short Stories

The Wait

Read More About Frances M. Thompson

Read Frankie's blog at www.asthebirdfliesblog.com

Find other books by Frances M. Thompson on Amazon, Kobo, Bookshop.org, and at www.ko-fi.com/birdswords. You can also rate and review this book, and others, on Goodreads.

Follow Frankie on Instagram - @asthebirdfliesblog – or on Twitter - @asthebirdflies.

And if you enjoyed this book, please do share your favourite poems on social media with #LoverMotherOtherPoems.

Printed in Great Britain
by Amazon